LEADERSHIP INSIGHTS

101 Principles to Increase Your Wisdom

LEADERSHIP INSIGHTS

101 Principles to Increase Your Wisdom

Bob BIEHL

Executive Mentor

Practical Wisdom
Leading • Managing • Living

Written permission must be secured from the publisher to use or reproduce any part of this book, except for brief quotations in critical reviews or articles. The Bible version used in this publication is THE NEW KING JAMES VERSION. Copyright © 1979, 1980, 1982, Thomas Nelson, Inc., Publishers.
Library of Congress Cataloging-in-Publication Data
Biehl, Bobb.

Published by Aylen Publishing
P.O. Box 1999
Mt. Dora, FL 32756

All rights reserved
Printed in the United States of America

Subject Heading: 1. Emotions. 2. Affect (Psychology) 3. Self-defeating behavior
ISBN 0-9765040-8-1

Leadership Insights

Leadership is . . .
　Leadership is
　Knowing WHAT to do next . . .
　Knowing WHY that is important . . . and,
　Knowing HOW to bring the appropriate resources to bear on the need at hand.

　Christian Leadership is
　Knowing WHAT Jesus would do next . . .
　Knowing WHY He would see this as important . . . and,
　Knowing HOW He would bring the appropriate resources to bear on the need at hand.

　　As a leader keep asking yourself . . .
　　What next? Why? Where will we get the resources?

Wisdom is . . .
　Whenever you approach a wise friend to seek wisdom . . .
　　he/she helps you . . .
　Know WHAT to do next . . .
　Know WHY that is important . . . and,
　Know HOW to bring the appropriate resources to bear on the need at hand.

Hundreds of Proven Principles
　In *Leadership Insights* you will find hundreds of principles that are born out of over thirty years of professional consulting experience. I have had the privilege of consulting with over 400 of the finest leaders of our generation. These proven principles come out of that experience.

I have a life collection of over 1,000 wise leadership principles . . . Leadership Insights has the top 101. Not all of these insights will lead to an immediate "AHA!" for you, but you never know which one will reveal something you have **never** before seen, heard, or thought, taking you and your team to a whole new leadership level. You can also use these wise principles for team exercises with your team or with individual team members.

A Quick Diagnostic

This list can also serve as a quick diagnostic. If you should ever feel "stuck" in knowing exactly what's wrong or where to go with your team, simply start down these Leadership, Management, and Life principles. More than likely, some principle will pop you out of the stuck feeling and speed you on your way!

24 x 7 x 365 x LIFE!

These insights can help bring fresh perspective to your thinking 24 hours a day, 7 days a week, 365 days a year for the rest of your life. They are designed to be timeless strengtheners for you and your team!

Here to help you win!

Bobb
BIEHL

1

| 10% RULE | How can you say what you are trying to say with 10% of the words, time, and money you are using?

This is a real "fog cutter" in all of your communications, proposals, speeches, literature, etc.

Simplify . . .
the fewer words we use
the more successful the result. |

2

60% RULE

Investing 60%
of your time on a project
does not
guarantee its success,
but
investing less than 60%
of your time on a project
(or managing someone who does)
guarantees its mediocrity.

Notice I didn't say failure.

You can seem to be successful
in many things at the same time,
as other people see you.

Each project
which receives less than 60% of your
time will only be mediocre
compared to what it could be
if you would focus on it.

What should be your 60% focus?

What should be the 60% focus
of each of your team members?

3

$20,000 / HOUR	To focus on your largest boulders fast, ask yourself, "What professional activity should I do that is worth $20,000 per hour?" And, "What activity I do is worth $20 per hour?" Then concentrate on the $20,000 activities and try to eliminate the $20 activities.

4

| ASSUMPTIONS | "All miscommunication is the result of differing assumptions!"
— *Dr. Jerry Ballard*

And, leads to frustration, pressure, and tension.

To get to the bottom of a frustrating situation fast, remember this quote.

Begin listing your assumptions.

Have your friend or staff member do the same.

Quickly, as you compare assumptions you will find where you have miscommunication and the source of your Frustration, Pressure, and Tension. |

5	
AUDIENCE OF ONE	"Live life with an audience of One (God)." – *Os Guinness*

6	
BALANCE	Life is a constant struggle for balance. Balance is a result of one word . . . schedule. Typically, you determine your own schedule. Therefore, you schedule your own balance / imbalance. Plan basic balance into your life by scheduling many of the really important things into your life (family vacations, personal retreats, time with parents, etc.) ONE YEAR in advance. At this point in your life . . . it may be the only way to achieve any semblance of balance!

BOULDERS	"What 3 things can we do in the next 90 days to make a 50% difference?" – Steve Douglass
	This question helps you spot the boulders in your life.
	Once you get the first 3 done there is always a next 3 for another quick 50%.
	You can also change the question by substituting 1 year, 5 years, 10 years, or life for the 90 day time frame to get a longer range picture of your future.

8	
BUMPER STICKER	Reducing your team's focus to a slogan that could go on a clever "bumper sticker" focuses your thinking and your communications!

9	
COMMITMENT —REALLY	Of all the things you have said you will do in the future . . . what do you "really mean"? What would you be willing to die for today? What would you be willing to give thirty-forty years of your life for—starting now?

10

COMMITMENT — "WINNING"	Are you focused on "Getting By" or, on "Winning Big!"?
	Losers don't focus on losing, they just focus on "Getting By."
	"Winning Big!" is often going an extra 10% in many cases.

11

CONDITIONS	"What would I have to do to be fired . . . to get a raise /bonus?" – *Ben Clark*

12 CONFIDENCE

Confidence is a byproduct of predictability.

No predictability . . . no confidence.

Lots of predictability . . . lots of confidence.

This principle is true in all areas of life . . .

> *Family/Marriage*
> *Financially*
> *Personal Growth*
> *Physically*
> *Professionally*
> *Socially*
> *Spiritually*

Lots of predictability = lots of confidence!
Little predictability = little confidence.

When your confidence becomes shaky . . . focus on what is very predictable in the situation.

Confidence comes back automatically.

13

| CONFRONTA-TION | If your approach moves from CONFRONTING to CLARIFYING . . . your anxiety level will drop dramatically.

Clarify your assumptions.
Clarify your expectations.

Nothing clarifies like measurability! |

14

CONTEXT	NOTHING is meaningful without a context or comparison.
	Comparable sales in the recent past is the context which gives meaning to your house valuation.
	A process chart is often the context for your search for meaning within various organizational issues, problems, and questions.
	Eternity past and future is the relevant context for our lives today.

15

CREDIBILITY	When your VISIBILITY exceeds your ABILITY it destroys your CREDIBILITY.

Are we really ready to grow?

WHAT IF . . .
we were to grow
five-ten (+) times faster
than we think in the next year?
How can we increase our ability
to keep from losing our credibility?

16

DECISIONS—FACTS

"Once the facts are clear, the decisions jump out at you."
— *Dr. Peter F. Drucker*

If
you are having a hard time
trying to make a key decision,
ask one simple question:

"What facts do I need
before
I can make a wise decision?"

When you have a lot of key decisions
facing you . . . make them line up
and
make your decisions one at a time
in priority order.

Don't try to solve them all at once.

17

| DECISIONS—SPEED | "Speed in making up one's mind is not an important element in successful choices.

In fact, the snap decision is often not a decision at all but a technique of avoidance.

Though it created an illusion of command, a lightning choice may mean only that someone has snatched at the handiest alternative rather than come to grips with the real issues involved."
        – *Dr. Joyce Brothers* |

18 DECISIONS— WISE

What are the three most critical decisions
you need to make *this year*?

What do you *have* to know
to make these decisions wisely?

These two questions
will focus your head quickly
and,
help you in focusing in on a wise decision!

Obviously, you can substitute the words
> week,
> month,
> quarter,

for "this year."

Be wise,
ask these questions often.
in the decision making process.

19

| DEFINING QUESTION | What
single
measurable
goal
do you want to reach *ten years* from today?

What will have to happen
for your team to reach
_____
in ten years?

How old will you be in ten years?

Today,
you are halfway between ten years ago
and
ten years from now!

In the past ten years
you have gained a world of experience
getting you ready
to grow into the challenges
of the next ten years! |

20 DELEGATION

When you are doing something
that someone else on your staff could do
80% as well,
you are probably wasting your time doing it.

Learning
to delegate effectively
is even more important
in determining the size of your contribution
in life
than your native intelligence.

Make a list
of all you have to do in the next ninety days.

You may also want
to ask your team members which
items on the list they feel confident
doing . . . consider delegating those
items to him/her.

Ask
what someone on your team
(paid or unpaid)
could do 80% as well as you could do it.
Consider delegating it.

21

DOUBT

"I spent a long time
trying to come to grips with my
doubts
and suddenly
I realized
that I had better come to grips with
what I
believe.

I have since moved
from the agony of questions
that I cannot answer,
to the reality of answers
that I cannot escape . . .
and
it's a great relief."
– *Tom Skinner*

DREAM—LIFE	What is my "Life Dream"?

Your "Life Dream"
is
the difference you hope to make with your life
sometime
before you die.

A "Life Dream"
is
what energizes the human spirit for decades
without
needing a lot of
outside encouragement / stimulation.

Once you define your "Life Dream"
ask yourself a second question.

"What are the
TEN CRITICAL STEPS
needed to turn my dream into reality?"

These two questions (combined)
 are very powerful
in helping create energy and direction
for the rest of your natural life! |

23

DREAM-SPARKING

Dream-sparking is asking the question,

> "If
> our team received a gift
> equal to
> THIS YEAR'S ENTIRE BUDGET,
> if we had to spend it all
> this year . . .
> what would we do with the money?"

This single question / exercise
helps your team
climb quickly to a "50,000 foot view"
of your entire organization
and
dream of its hypothetically possible future!

Imagining the future
is harder
for some than others.
But,
with this imaginary question
everyone stretches their minds about the future.

It is a stretching question.

24

DRIVING FORCE	Assign any major new project to one person to be its DRIVING FORCE at least 60% (See #2 – 60% rule) of his/her time or the project should be stopped, postponed, or reconsidered as a priority. When you start something, consider stopping/postponing something else. Be cautious about a situation where you just keep adding.

25

| DRUCKER'S PROFOUND QUESTIONS | "Who are our CUSTOMERS?

What do they NEED?

Therefore, what BUSINESS are we in?"

– *Dr. Peter F. Drucker* |

26

DRY LEAVES

When
you are taking on impossible odds
start with the "Dry Leaves"...
the handful
who are eager to help you in your mission!

Boy scouts
have a concept called the "one match fire."

If,
you are lost in a rain soaked forest...
don't use the one dry match you have left
to try and ignite a huge rain soaked log.

Look for some dry leaves...
pile on a few damp twigs...
then some wet branches...
and, eventually this blaze can start
even a large
rain soaked log.

Who
are the "Dry Leaves"
people,
clients,
projects,
donors, etc.
... in your world?

27

| EFFECTIVENESS | "Efficiency
is
doing things right.

Effectiveness
is
doing right things."
– Dr. Peter F. Drucker |

28

| EFFICIENCY | "What do you
Have
to know
to do what you
Have
to do?"
– *Sy Simington*

This
one question
is a "fog cutter"
of the first order.

It clears away all of the "Possibilities"
and "What if's" . . . the "Options" . . .
and
focuses on . . .
"What we *HAVE* to know
     to do what we *HAVE* to do!" |

29

ENCOURAGEMENT

When
your team is discouraged . . . STOP
and
focus on your past MILESTONES!

99% of the time
your team
will move quickly from feeling
discouraged
to feeling encouraged.

This
is the fastest way I know of lifting
team spirit!

Today,
make a list of past milestones
with your team.

You will find the list helpful in
"evening out" your team's ups and
downs.

Whenever
you feel yourself
tiring in life's up-the-mountain
climb . . . stop . . . look back . . .
make a list of your personal
milestones . . .
you will feel encouraged personally!

30

FOUR LEVELS OF THINKING	Level 1. Everyone *is* like me. Level 2. Everyone *is not* like me. Level 3. *No one* is like me. Level 4. It is *OK* to be me. Level four clarity often comes to a person at about age thirty-five. Level four clarity is also key to building your team. It is critical to find each person's strength and maximize it, rather than insist that he/she be like you!

31

FUN	Fun is "uninhibited spontaneity." Things that are inhibited and not spontaneous seem boring. Think back to the last time you were having fun. Why was it so much fun? The activity was uninhibited and spontaneous. Your team needs a bit of fun. Occasionally it is important to relax and let your team flow in an uninhibited and spontaneous "fun" way!

32

HAPPINESS

Happiness
is
having what you want
and
wanting what you have.

By focusing your thinking
on what you have
that you
want,
you'll be a lot happier
than focusing your thinking
on what you want
but don't have.

33

HEART

"When you meet a man
you judge him by his clothes . . .
when you leave a man you judge him
by his
heart."
— *An Ancient Russian Proverb*

How do you see people?

34	
HUMAN RELATIONS	If you have two basically equal companies, the company with the best Human Relations / Personnel Department wins long-term! Small / Start-up companies assume "better anyone than no one." Wise companies assume "better no one than the wrong one." Screening carefully in the "hiring" process avoids many staff problems and avoids many "firing" type problems later.

35

IDEAL	What would be the "ideal" solution long-term?
	This one profound question can save your team hours of discussion.
	Simply asking the "ideal" question moves any and all discussions away from the immediate realities (people, budgets etc.) to the highest level possible.
	This one question is a "fog cutter" of the first order.

36 IF

"If I had _____
I would _____."
— *Moshe Rosen*

The exercise of filling out these two blanks is a
real "fog cutter" for you to use in nearly any
situation.

Ask your team to fill in the blanks
"If we had

_____

we would

_____."

Try it . . .
don't just read it and smile.

This is an exercise
you can do several times per year,
yourself or with your team.

It is also a great exercise
to do with your spouse / parents /
children.

37

IF— ANYTHING

"If,
you could do anything you wanted,
if God
told you that you were free to choose,
and
you had all the time,
money,
staff,
and education you wanted
and,
you knew for certain you could not fail . . .
what would you actually do?"
— *Bob Walker*

I have asked this question
of leaders at least 500 times.
It is a very proven "fog cutter"
question.

You may think
everyone knows this question
and
has been asked to answer it time and time again.
Not true!
It seems brand new to 99% of the people I've asked this question!

38

**IF—
BEFORE YOU
DIE**

If,
you could only accomplish
three measurable things
before you die,
what three things would you
accomplish?

This question is a very helpful
question to ask
anyone in a foggy phase of life.

Give yourself,
a friend,
a team member
EXACTLY TWO MINUTES
to answer.

You will be surprised
at how many people can give you a
crystal clear answer to the question
asked this way.

This one exercise
will give you crystal clear insight
into what is really important
to the person.
And,
clarifies in the person's mind
what is important to him/her
at a totally new level.

39

| IF—
YOU WERE
PRESIDENT | If,
you were made president
of our organization
today
what are the first three things you would do?

Why
would you do them?

These questions move anyone
immediately
to a 50,000 foot view of your
organization.

They allow you to see
which of your team members thinks
naturally/easily
at the big picture level.

And,
it helps get a person ready
to be president
when the time comes. |

40

IN / ON

"What percentage of your time
are you working
IN (building a high quality product/service)
your organization
and, what percentage of your time
are you working
ON (building a high quality company)
it?"

– *Bobby Albert*

The lower level workers in a firm
are typically working "in" the
company. The higher you go in your
company the higher the percentage of
your time that
should be invested working "on" the
company.

Decide today,
at this phase of your career,
how much of your time per week
should you spend working "on" the
company.
Then
block it out, schedule it in, stick to it!

The company will be a lot stronger
in the long run.

41

INFORMAL RESEARCH	You can learn *80%* (approximately) of what you need to know about a subject by asking the right ten people the right ten questions in less than ten minutes each.
	The other *20%* of what you need to know takes $100,000+ for formal research.
	Test before you invest.
	Before you start investing large dollars, ask a few prospective buyers...
	"Would you buy this product/service for $_____?" If eight out of ten people say, "No!" keep looking. If eight out of ten people say, "Yes!" you're probably on the right track!

42

LEADERSHIP— ENEMIES

The three enemies of great leadership are:

1. **Fog** . . . Because even a brand new Ferrari can only go about two miles an hour safely in a dense fog. With a "foggy" brain you can't begin to realize your natural "horsepower." The quicker you clear your head, the quicker you can be at full throttle mentally!

2. **Fatigue** . . . According to the late great Green Bay Packers coach Vince Lombardi, "Fatigue . . . makes cowards of us all." It also turns us introspective/negative. Fatigue warps our objectivity in decision making. Avoid making a critical decision when fatigued. Whenever a person says, "I'm really tired," start listening and encouraging. If you try to sell and convince a fatigued person, you will only overwhelm and alienate.

3. **Flirtations** . . . When you are in a "fog" . . . become fatigued . . . you are tempted to flirt with a wide variety of ideas with which you should not be flirting.

43

LEADERSHIP IS	Leadership is Knowing WHAT to do next . . . Knowing WHY that is important . . . and, Knowing HOW to bring the appropriate resources to bear on the need at hand. Christian Leadership is Knowing WHAT Jesus would do next . . . Knowing WHY He would see this as important . . . and, Knowing HOW He would bring the appropriate resources to bear on the need at hand. As a leader keep asking yourself . . . What next? Why? Where will we get the resources? If you ask fifty people to define leadership you will get forty-nine different definitions. The above definition has held true in all organizations, at all levels, and in all countries for our team for over thirty years.

44

LEADERSHIP— KEY ELEMENTS

85% (approximately) of leadership (from a
human perspective) is:

1. Clear direction
2. The right team
3. Enough money

My book, *Masterplanning*,
calls these three
Direction, Organization, and Cash.

I have asked many wise experienced leaders
if this 85% principle made sense to them.
They usually pause,
remembering various assignments over decades, and
typically answer either,

"At least 85%"
or,
"85% is probably low."

Whenever you feel in a leadership fog
... focus on DOC:
1. Direction – clear direction
2. Organization – the right team
3. Cash – enough money

45

| LEADERSHIP STAR | The five points of the Leadership Star are:
　　CARE,
　　HONEST,
　　FAIR,
　　STRENGTHS, and
　　STRESS.

Whenever dealing with a team member you want these five questions in the front of your mind.

CARE – Do I really care about this person?
HONEST – Am I being honest with this person?
FAIR – Am I treating this person fairly?
STRENGTHS – Are we maximizing this person's strengths?
STRESS – Is there anything we can do to reduce this person's stress level?

A team can adjust to nearly any bad news if they feel that:
　• You truly care about them
　• You are being totally honest with them
　• You are treating them fairly

The "rocks hit the fan" if any one is missing. |

46

LIFE MESSAGE	If, you could stand on a platform for fifteen minutes talking to every person alive, and every person could hear you in his/her native tongue or through translators . . . what would you tell them? This one question helps focus your "LIFE MESSAGE!"

47

LIFEWORK

Your "LifeWork"
is the activity that is worthy
of the time, energy, and money
you have left in life.

Often a person (age thirty-five to
fifty) feels a restlessness of
heart and starts asking questions like:

> "Should I change jobs?"
> "What is my career path?"
> "What is my future?"

What the heart is actually seeking is a
"LifeWork."

A "LifeWork" can give a person
a single/stable direction for ten–sixty
years!

48

MASTERPLAN

A masterplan
is
a written statement
of a group's assumptions
about its direction,
its organization,
and its cash.

Ideally,
a masterplan is no longer than three-five pages, but on those three-five pages one finds
several hundred assumptions.

When each team member
reads the masterplan
he/she can spot areas of question
or disagreement.
When discussions have been held
and
questions have been answered,
your entire team
starts playing off the "same sheet of music."

Team Harmony.

49

MEMORY GRID

Anything
you have read 100 times
you have memorized
whether you planned to or not.

Highlight the wisdom in this book you would like to memorize.

When you are sitting in a doctor's office waiting
or
have an unexpected fifteen–sixty minutes free,
read and re-read them.

When you have read each one 100 times,
you have memorized them
whether you planned to or not.

50

MENTORING

Ideally,
mentoring is a lifelong relationship
in which the mentor
helps the protégé
realize his/her God given potential.

Mentoring
is a key to acceleration in one's career.
And,
offers protection for the protégé
on the mountain of life.

The mentoring time is focused with two
questions asked by the mentor:

> "What are your plans?"
> "How can I help?"

For a fuller understanding of the subject of
mentoring, visit www.Aylen.com.

51

| MOMENTUM | "CONSIDER that you are in a war to 'CREATE EVIDENCE'— evidence that you are winning, that the strategy is succeeding, that you are building momentum.

Fighting against you in this war will be fault-finders who are recording every misfire and telling everyone who will listen.

You need evidence to help you gain the genuine support of your colleagues."
– *Christopher Zikakis*

Do not communicate false hype. Communicate actual results clearly and frequently! |

52

MONEY

When you can't figure out exactly what's going on in an organization,
watch where the money goes . . .
how it flows step-by-step . . .
from the time it comes in until it goes out.

You may be surprised.

53

NATURAL EXCITEMENT	What are you *really*, *really*, *really* (yes, you need to repeat really three times) excited about today? This is a non-threatening but very profound question to ask any person, any where, at any time to get a quick look at what's in the person's heart. It is actually a good party question. It is also a great question to ask each team member over lunch, dinner, or as a team discussion. It is also a good question to have the team ask itself as a group. What are we as a team *really*, *really*, *really* excited about today?

54

NEEDS

There are eight reasons why people do what they do. These are insatiable needs. They are the needs to be:
- ❏ Loved
- ❏ Significant
- ❏ Admired
- ❏ Recognized
- ❏ Appreciated
- ❏ Secure
- ❏ Respected
- ❏ Accepted

We all need all of these.

But, different individuals rate them very differently on a 1-10 scale. What a husband rates a "10" may be a "3" to his wife . . . and, vice versa.

The same with individual team members. What really motivates you may not motivate your team members at all.

Each need has a very predictable pattern of fears, styles, strengths, back up styles, etc. connected with it. This model is very helpful in motivating your entire team. The model is fully explained in the book *Why You Do What You Do*, and is available at www.Aylen.com.

55

| NEGOTIATION | Negotiating
typically implies
"more for me...less for you!"

Never negotiate.

Always work toward a "triple win!"
where at least three of the parties (all parties) involved
come away "winning!" |

56

| NEW NORMAL | When major change comes to most people,
they keep waiting for things to
"get back to normal."

When this "I just want it the way it used to be"
feeling hits you,
a team member,
or someone you love,
remember the phrase . . .

"This is the New Normal."

It really helps in the adjustment to difficult new realities. |

57

NEW POSITION

What
do you really want to
preserve,
avoid, and
achieve?

When you are being considered
for a new position,
let the recruiter/manager/committee
ask any and all questions they care to ask.

Then ask if you can ask them a question:

"What
do you really want to
PRESERVE,
AVOID, and
ACHIEVE?"

If,
you will keep digging into their
answers
to this one question,
it will become clear to you if this is a
challenge
you care to accept.

Always,
ask this question before accepting any
new position (paid or unpaid).

58

NOTHING	Nothing *ENERGIZES* like a dream
	Nothing *CLARIFIES* like measurability
	Nothing *INTENSIFIES* like reducing the time to the target
	Nothing *MOTIVATES* like results!
	These are four "NOTHINGS" you can count on for the rest of your life!

59

OPPORTUNITY

"Last year's
unexpected success
is next year's
opportunity."
— *Dr. Peter F. Drucker*

The reason
it was unexpectedly successful
was the fact that you and your team
underestimated this area's
potential.

Have each person on your team
identify what surprised him/her
with how successful the last year has
been . . .
then ask each:

> "How can we take full advantage
> of this opportunity
> to make this area ten times as
> successful
> next year?"

Expect resistance.
People generally resist the change that
growth demands.

60

ORGANIZATION	Organization is having a place for everything and everything in its place.
	This definition is a "Grandma and Grandpa" type definition. But, it is true just the same.
	Whenever you are feeling disorganized it is because things are out of place or don't have a place.
	Organization is far more important to some team members than others.
	But, a form of organization is important to everyone.
	Discuss organization as a team.
	Come to a proper balance here.

61

ORGANIZATION —PERSONAL

There are four tools you need to feel personally organized:

1. A "To Do" List
2. A Calendar
3. An Address Book
4. A File System

These four tools can be on your computer or on the back of a 3 x 5 card . . . but, you need these four tools.

1. **Your "To Do" List . . .** is simply a prioritized list of the things you need to get done.
2. **Your Calendar . . .** depending on how you need to keep track of time can be yearly . . . monthly . . . weekly . . . daily . . . minutes. A calendar is for keeping track of specific time dated commitments.
3. **Your Address Book . . .** keeps track of your friends, vendors, suppliers, and network!
4. **Your File System . . .** keeps track of the items you want to save for the future in an organized, easy to retrieve way.

It is important to see that each person differs in how they like to keep organized. Find a way that is your own style . . . your own system. Learn from others but figure out what works for you.

62

PASSION	"What is your natural passion?" – Chuck Swindoll
	What is your passion today, not five years ago . . . or five years from now?
	Today, what makes you weep or pound the table?
	Caution . . . don't make long-term commitments based on current passion. Today's passion can pass and you are left with a long-term responsibility.

63

PEAKING

Plan to "peak" ten years from today.

And, each year on your birthday move it out a year. On your fiftieth birthday, plan to peak at age sixty. On your eightieth birthday, plan to peak at age ninety!

The vast majority of my clients are shocked to learn that very wealthy individuals say the decades in which they made the very most money were as follows:

Sixties—the very most profitable decade;
Seventies—the second most profitable decade;
Fifties—the third most profitable decade.

This insight often brings great relief to leaders in their thirties and forties who have not "made a fortune yet."

For Christian workers and other non-profit leaders the same logic holds, but instead of financial profit that peaks in the sixties, you can substitute words like influence, respect, significance, impact, etc.

Keep growing!

64

PERSPECTIVE—INTELLIGENCE	Perspective is worth fifty IQ points.
	You
	can be brilliant
	and
	have some really "goofy thinking"
	if
	you lose perspective.
	If is far better
	to be wise
	than brilliant.
	Promotions
	are given to the wise not the brilliant.
	King Solomon's age-old advice is
	"Seek
	Wisdom"!

65

| PERSPECTIVE—LIFE | You are God's student,
not
life's victim!

Teach your children and your team
to learn from each hurt.

Teach your children and your team
that all disappointment
is
actually
God's protection

Teach your children and your team
that each is God's student—
growing and becoming
what He has in mind for them to
be/do
someday! |

66

PERSPECTIVE—ORGANIZATION

"Where have we been?
Where are we?
Where are we going?"
— *Dr. Ted W. Engstrom*

Dr. Engstrom was chairman of the board of a major university. The board invited a major consulting firm for an eighteen month consultation.

The first month the consultant announced the discussions that day would be on the questions:
"Where have we been?
Where are we now?
Where are we going?"

At day's end they felt great progress.

The next month the consultant returned and again announced the discussions that day would be on the questions:
"Where have we been?
Where are we now?
Where are we going?"

This happened for eighteen months in a row.

I've heard Dr. Engstrom ask many times, "What do you think our board truly understood at the end of the eighteen months?"

67

| PERSPECTIVE— SUBJECTIVITY | To a hammer everything looks like a nail. Be careful you don't see everything through the glasses of your "pet agenda." |

68

PLANNING—APPROACHES

There are three approaches to planning:

1. **Goal setters' approach** . . . all planning begins at the end . . . begin with the end in mind . . . and, work backwards toward today.

2. **Problem solvers' approach** . . . solve what's in front of you . . . or tomorrow won't come true anyway.

3. **Opportunity oriented approach** . . . planning is building capacity to respond to opportunity . . . and, removing any roadblocks keeping us from opportunity.

Which approach do you *actually* prefer?

Which approach is the most *naturally energizing* to you?

Which approach
is most naturally energizing for each of your
team members . . .
your spouse . . .
your children . . .
the other leaders in your life?

69

POLICY

Policy
is
what we always do
or,
what we never do.

For example . . .

Financial policy is what we always do,
or never do,
when it comes to money.

Personnel policy is what we
always do,
or never do,
when it comes to personnel.

A typical organization
rarely has more than a dozen
carefully crafted policy statements
at the board level.

But,
each department or division
may have its own dozen or so policies.

70 PREPARATION

"If you knew, by divine revelation, that you were going to be president of your organization in five years, what would you have to *know, do*, or *become* to feel/be ready?"
– *Mary Graham*

It is never too early to spot future presidents and get them ready.

It is never too early to get in mind what you would do if your current leader were taken unexpectedly.

> **Caution:** Be careful about telling anyone they will someday be president . . . things change!

But, you may want to be getting one to three people ready,
via training, to become president of this
or another organization if called upon to do so.

For information on the Bobb Biehl Leadership
Academy (presidential preparation), visit
www.Aylen.com.

71

PRIORITIES

"If,
you are Noah
and the ark is sinking . . .
look for the elephants first!"
— *Preto*

You could throw over hundreds
of smaller animals
and the ark would just keep sinking.
But,
if you could just throw one
elephant overboard
the side of the boat would come up a
long way.

Point:

In your budget,
you could cut a lot of items by 10–
50%
and still be in very deep trouble
financially.

But,
if you look at the three
largest expenses
and cut a small percentage of
these areas,
it would make a huge difference.

72

| PROBLEMS—HUGE | What one huge problem are you dealing with that you would happily pay 10% of your annual budget to have solved for you?

Be careful not to dismiss this question with a quick "nothing is worth 10% of our budget!"

How much would you be willing to pay if someone could show you realistically how to triple your income? Reduce expenses by half?

This is actually an outstanding brainstorming question.

What would be worth 10% of your budget to you today? |

73

PROBLEMS—SOLUTIONS

"Bring me
options and solutions
not problems."
— *Paul Weaver*

This principle
is extremely helpful,
especially in working with young
staff.

Ask each of
your team members to bring you
three optional solutions,
with his/her final recommendation
and reasons
on a single sheet of paper.

This exercise helps to:

- Develop your team members
- Show you who has great ideas / judgment
- Save you hours of time

And, it is good leadership modeling
for your entire team.

74

| QUESTIONS | If you ask *profound* questions,   you get profound answers!

If you ask *shallow* questions,   you get shallow answers!

If you ask no questions,   you get *no* answers at all!

Collect "fog cutting" questions for a lifetime. |

75

RAW REALITY	If, we just look at "raw reality" where are we? What do the numbers say? What does the bank account say? What would we do if we had to decide in the next two minutes? How do we best balance this raw reality with our dreams? What are the first three steps we could take to move us from this raw reality to a more hopeful phase? Just as realistic . . . what are the positive steps we have taken in the past thirty to ninety days?

76

REPORTING QUESTIONS

Once your priorities (measurable problems, goals, opportunities) are clear, these reporting questions will keep you and your team focused on the boulders:

** 1. What DECISIONS do you need from me?

** 2. What PROBLEMS are keeping you from your priorities?

* 3. What PLANS are you making (which haven't been discussed)?

* 4. What PROGRESS have you made? (numbers, charts, trends, etc.)

** 5. On a scale of 1-100, how are you PERSONALLY? Why?

(Optional – for Christian organizations)

* 6. How can I PRAY for you?

* These areas are best covered in staff meetings
** These areas are best 1:1 or with select team members who are directly affected by the discussion

Ideally, all reports should be on a single page.

77

ROCKET	What is our "ROCKET"?
	What is the one project/program/tool/service that everyone likes?
	If it "sells well" everything else sells far better.
	If this one item goes "into orbit" it takes everything else with it!
	Give your "rocket" all of the fuel (budget) it can use effectively!
	You may want to make a list of all of your projects/programs/tools/services, and then have your team rate each as:
	10 = drives all the sales 1 = drives nothing but its own sales
	See which element of your organization is really driving (or, has the potential to drive) everything else . . . focus here!

78

| ROOT CAUSE | Focus on cause elimination, not symptom reduction.

What is the root cause of our current problem? |

79

| SINGLE GREATEST STRENGTH | What is your "SINGLE GREATEST STRENGTH"?

What do you DO the very BEST?

There may be many things you do "better than most." But, which do you do the "very best"?

What does each member of your team do the very best? It is your responsibility to maximize that strength.

Focus on maximizing your strength, not eliminating your weakness! |

80

SINGLE WORD FOCUS

What single word
captures
the essence of your life's direction,
organization's focus,
next year's focus,
sermon,
speech,
chapter,
or presentation?

The single-word-focus is
one of my most trusted "fog-cutters"!

For example,
when the founder of the
Salvation Army,
General William Booth,
was offered one word
to be transmitted worldwide via
telegraph, he simply sent, "Others!"

When you ask your brain
what single word best expresses
what you are trying to say/do,
often your brain gives you
a single word answer in seconds.

This single word
focuses your thinking/planning
and
can save you hours of
preparation time.

81

SOMEDAY

"Someday _____ (person/organization)

will be a world class _____!"

This simple exercise can help you define a person's strengths in a matter of seconds.

This includes your own strengths. Fill it in for yourself.

"Someday I
want to be a world class
_____!"

Use this exercise
to help identify/define strengths
of individuals on your team (paid/unpaid),
and
among your family/friends.
It is a great "fog cutter"!

| STORY | "What is the story
that has magic . . .
a magic title/headline
needs to come out of the
magic story."
— *Bill McKendry*

What story in your work
touches you in a way that you
can also see
touches the audience?

What story moves people to action?

What story touches the heart?

What story drives home your point?

What is the key phrase
in the story
that should become a headline/title? |

83

| STRATEGIC DIRECTION | "A business can tolerate a truly enormous number of errors in detail if the strategic direction is relevant and correct."
— Mr. Richard S. Sloma

Keep remembering your DREAM
(The difference you hope to make before you die)

Keep remembering your PRIMARY RESULT
(The single best measurable indicator that you are moving toward your dream)

Keep remembering your PROCESSES
(The step-by-step way you are moving toward your primary result)

One mile per hour in the right direction beats 100 miles per hour in the wrong direction any day! |

84

STRENGTH

"The role of an organization is
to maximize the strength
of the individual
and
make the individual's weakness irrelevant."
— *Dr. Peter F. Drucker*

This is a profound quote which is actually a
solid management philosophy.

Many leaders ask,
"Are we getting our money's worth
out of this team member?"
This is the wrong question.
The question should be,
"How do we maximize this person's unique strength?"

This is actually one of the central principles we teach at the Consulting Institute.

For more information about the
Consulting Institute,
visit www.ConsultingInstitute.com.

85

STRESS

As much as 80%
of all stress
is caused by
indecision
or
lack of control.

If,
you are under great stress today
ask yourself two questions:

1. What are the three main things in your life that are out of control?

2. What are the three primary decisions you have to make in the next six months?

Focus on these areas.

Any progress you
or your team
makes in getting these areas
under control,
or
making these decisions wisely, will
start reducing your stress level.

86

STYLE

When someone is doing something in a way
that displeases you . . .
you need to ask yourself
if the way they are doing it is:

ILLEGAL (against the law)

IMMORAL (against an absolute moral code)

UNETHICAL (against local business practices) or just a

STYLE that is different than yours.

Relax
with stylistic differences
in the way your team handles things.

But,
pay careful attention
if you see a team member doing something that
is
ILLEGAL,
IMMORAL, or
UNETHICAL!

87

| SYSTEMS | "Double the strength of the weakest link in a chain and you double the reliability of the entire chain."
— *Ed Gruman*

What is the weakest "critical link" in the chain of your organization, from introduction to the final product/service?

Focus on doubling its strength, and see its impact on the end result.

What would the implications be to your entire organization if you were to double the strength of the weakest link, and— in fact—double the strength of your entire organizational chain? |

88

TIME	"Your true adversary is time; not competition, not legislation, not the economy, but time." – *Richard S. Sloma* Focus on time and you will win the competition far more often.

89

TIMING—GOD'S	God's timing is perfect, even when it differs from our plans. In God's sovereignty, He is never a nanosecond too early or too late.

90

TIMING—WHEN

"It's
not
what you know.

It's
not
who you know.

It's
when
you know it."
— Ed Orr

Whenever
you hear reliable news/information
from your network of friends,
ask yourself . . .

"What does this *mean*?"

"What are the *implications* of this information?"

"Where in here can I find *unexpected opportunity*?"

It's when you know it!

91

TOOLS

"Any
tool
a man needs in his business
he is paying for,
whether he has it
or not."
— *John H. Patterson*

Let's say
you need a hammer
and don't have one.

You lose business
day after day
because you can't drive in nails.

You are paying for
not having
the screwdriver
through lost business
just as realistically as if you had paid
for a screwdriver.

92

| TRANSITIONS | Transition is a phase in which major encouragement needs to be your focus as a leader.

In the middle of a transition, keep your team focused on their progress and the opportunities this transition represents.

Every transition causes an increase in the stress level (there is a predictable increase in stress because of increased indecision and lack of control), even though it may also represent major new opportunities for you and your team as well. |

93

TRENDS	"Don't only watch the trends, watch the changes in the trends." — Dr. Peter F. Drucker

TRENDS (continued)

Let's say
your event attendance
has been going up at a rate of
5% per year
for the past ten years . . .
but this year it changed to 25%.
Stop and ask yourself:

"What does this *trend increase* mean?"

"What are the *implications* of this trend increase?"

"Where in this trend increase can we find *unexpected opportunity*?"

Watch the changes in your trends!

94

TURN AROUND

To turn an organization around
in thirty days . . .

> **hire** one desperately needed person,
>
> **fire** one visible problematic person,
>
> **stop** something everyone on the team knows should have stopped long ago.

The bottom line
may not turn around in thirty days,
but
the team morale will,
and
profits should be very close behind!

95

UNIQUENESS	What is our unique market/ministry position?
	What can we do that others can't?
	How can we maximize our positive uniqueness?
	People will pay extra for what they want but can't get anywhere else.
	Feature your uniqueness in your advertising and all of your signage.

96

| VISION | "My
first responsibility
as a leader
is to see . . .
for if I can't see
I'm like
the blind
leading the blind."
— *John H. Patterson*

The higher
you are
in the organization,
the higher
the percentage of your time that
needs to be devoted to clear vision/
direction.

At this phase
of your team's development,
what percentage of your time
needs to be devoted to
keeping the team's vision crystal
clear? |

97

VISUAL PERSPECTIVE

Draw a picture of how you are feeling right now. This gives you "visual perspective" and can snap your "fog" into focus very quickly!

TAKE TEN MINUTES RIGHT NOW:

- Get a flip chart sized piece of paper if possible
- Draw a stick figure in the middle of the sheet
- Then, around the stick figure, draw all of the questions, pressures, opportunities, decisions, etc. that you are dealing with today
- Underline some of the areas several times to indicate critical importance
- Circle some in red to indicate danger
- Add your own creative art effects to help you visualize your life as you see it today

If you decided to share what you have just created with a close friend . . . would they have an accurate visual perspective of where you are at the moment? This is a tool you can use with staff, relatives, friends, and many others over the course of your entire lifetime.

I have proven it works!

98

VITAL SIGNS

What
are the seven vital signs of the
health
of our
organization?

These seven vital signs
are what the board should be
tracking regularly to make sure the
organization remains healthy.

Graph these seven vital signs:

- ❏ Plot the actual numbers from the past three years (relevant history), and
- ❏ Indicate (with dotted line) where the seven vital signs trends would go if the same percentage of growth or decline persisted, over the next ten years, as it has the past three years.

It will take your board, your senior executives,
and
your executive team
about five minutes
to see many of the organizational
implications of these seven
vital trend lines.

99

VISUALS	A picture is worth 1,000 words, and to a visionary, a graph or chart is worth 10,000 numbers.
	Use visuals when working with visionaries.
	Visionaries have an intuitive understanding of the implications of trends.
	When working with accountants and actuaries, include actual numbers.
	A chart/graph is a context which gives each new number meaning by its very context.
	Each dot on the chart is a whole new story.

100

WANT	What do you really want from life? IN MY LIFE I WANT TO . . .				
	BE	DO	HAVE	HELP	LEAVE
1					
2					
3					
4					
5					
6					
7					
8					
9					
10					

You will want to re-create this chart on a much larger sheet of paper—as large as you want. Write it in pencil or on your computer for easy updating. Keep it as a focusing chart for a lifetime.

When filled out you may ask, "What is the single most important item in each list of ten?" . . . circle it! You are getting pretty close to what is really, really, really important to you in your
life. That's why it is called the "I WANT CHART!"

101

WORK	An activity is work . . . only when you would rather be doing something else.
	Ideally, the way a person makes a living does not actually seem like "work."
	Ideally, the way you make your living is the kind of thing you would do if no one paid you to do it.
	Ideally, in hiring a team member, what they want to do in life should be what you have for them to do. To them it is not "work," but a pleasurable way to provide for their family.
	This may sound idealistic . . . If you will take the time needed in the hiring process and wait until the right person is in front of you, it is actually realistic!

Quoting

You have permission to quote up to three items from this list without written permission. Unless otherwise noted, all of the material in this handout is by Bobb Biehl. As you copy items please show source credit as:

Bobb Biehl - www.BobbBiehl.com.

Thank you!

Bobb
BIEHL

© 2008 Bobb Biehl • www.BobbBiehl.com • (800) 443-1976

Appendix A – Leadership Insights – List to Carry
Appendix B – Bobb Biehl – Leadership / Management Life Tools
Appendix C – Introduction to the Consulting Institute
Appendix D – Introduction to the Leadership Academy
Appendix E – Introduction to Consulting Services
Appendix F – Introduction to QuickWisdom

TEAR THE FOLLOWING 101 PRINCIPLES OUT OF THE BOOK.

Carry them with you . . . read them 100 times until they are committed to memory.

They will strengthen you for the rest of your life.

Leadership Insights

1 10% RULE
How can you say what you are trying to say with 10% of the words, time, and money you are using?

2 60% RULE
Investing 60% of your time on a project does not guarantee its success, but investing less than 60% of your time in a project (or managing someone who does) guarantees its mediocrity.

3 $20,000 / HOUR
To focus on your largest boulders fast, ask yourself what professional activity you do that is worth $20,000 per hour.

4 ASSUMPTIONS
"All miscommunications are the result of differing assumptions," according to Dr. Jerry Ballard . . . and lead to frustration, pressure, and tension.

5 AUDIENCE OF ONE
"Live life with an audience of One (God)."
— Os Guinness

6 BALANCE
Life is a constant struggle for balance. Balance is a result of one word . . . schedule. Typically you determine your own schedule. Therefore, you schedule your own balance/imbalance.

7 BOULDERS
"What 3 things can we do in the next 90 days to make a 50% difference?"   — Steve Douglass

8 BUMPER STICKER
Reducing your team's focus to a slogan that could go on a clever "bumper sticker" focuses your thinking and your communications!

9 COMMITMENT—REALLY
Of all the things you have said you will do in the future . . . what do you "really mean"?

10 COMMITMENT—"WINNING"
Are you focused on "Getting By" or on "Winning Big!"?

11 CONDITIONS
"What would I have to do to be fired . . . to get a raise?"   — Ben Clark

12 CONFIDENCE
Confidence is a byproduct of predictability.

13 CONFRONTATION
If your approach moves from CONFRONTING to CLARIFYING your anxiety will drop dramatically.

14 CONTEXT
Nothing is meaningful without context.

15 CREDIBILITY
When your visibility exceeds your ability, it destroys your credibility.

16 DECISIONS—FACTS
"Once the facts are clear, the decisions jump out at you."   — Dr. Peter F. Drucker

17 DECISIONS—SPEED
"Speed in making up one's mind is not an important element in successful choices. In fact, the snap decision is often not a decision at all but a technique of avoidance. Though it created an illusion of command, a lightning choice may mean only that someone has snatched at the handiest alternative rather than come to grips with the real issues involved."   — Dr. Joyce Brothers

18 DECISIONS—WISE
What are the three most critical decisions you need to make this year and what do you have to know to make these decisions wisely?

19 DEFINING QUESTION
What single measurable goal do you want to reach ten years from today? What has to happen for your team to reach _____ in ten years?

20 DELEGATION
When you are doing something that someone else on your staff could do 80% as well, you are probably wasting your time.

21 DOUBT
"I spent a long time trying to come to grips with my doubts and suddenly I realized that I had better come to grips with what I believe. I have since moved from the agony of questions that I cannot answer, to the reality of answers that I cannot escape . . . and it's a great relief."   — Tom Skinner

22 DREAM—LIFE
What is your "Life Dream"? Your "Life Dream" is the difference you hope to make sometime before you die. What are the TEN CRITICAL STEPS needed to turn your dream into reality?

23 DREAM-SPARKING
"Dream-sparking" is asking the question, "If our team received a gift/inheritance equal to THIS YEAR'S ENTIRE BUDGET, AS A SINGLE GIFT. . . if we had to spend it all this year . . . what would we do with the money?"

24 DRIVING FORCE
Assign any major new project to one person to be its DRIVING FORCE at least 60% of his/her time or the project should be stopped, postponed, or reconsidered as a priority.

25 DRUCKER'S PROFOUND QUESTIONS
"Who are our CUSTOMERS? What do they NEED? Therefore, what BUSINESS are we in?"
— Dr. Peter F. Drucker

26 DRY LEAVES
When you are taking on impossible odds, start with the "Dry Leaves"... the handful who are eager to help you in your mission!

27 EFFECTIVENESS
"Efficiency is doing things right. Effectiveness is doing right things."   – Dr. Peter F. Drucker

28 EFFICIENCY
"What do you Have to know to do what you Have to do?"   – Sy Simington

29 ENCOURAGEMENT
When your team is discouraged... STOP and focus on your past MILESTONES.

30 FOUR LEVELS OF THINKING
Level 1. Everyone is like me.
Level 2. Everyone is not like me.
Level 3. No one is like me.
Level 4. It is OK to be me.

31 FUN
Fun is "uninhibited spontaneity."

32 HAPPINESS
Happiness is having what you want and wanting what you have.

33 HEART
"When you meet a man you judge him by his clothes... when you leave a man you judge him by his heart."- An Ancient Russian Proverb

34 HUMAN RELATIONS
If you have two basically equal companies, the company with the best H.R. department wins long-term!

35 IDEAL
What would be the ideal solution long-term?

36 IF
"If I had _____ I would _____ _____."   – Moshe Rosen

37 IF—ANYTHING
If you could do anything you wanted, if God told you that you were free to choose and you had all the time, money, staff, and education, and you knew for certain you could not fail... what would you actually do?   – Bob Walker

38 IF—BEFORE YOU DIE
If you could only accomplish three measurable things before you die, what three things would you accomplish?

39 IF—YOU WERE PRESIDENT
If you were made president of your organization today what are the first three things you would do? Why would you do them?

40 IN / ON
"What percentage of your time are you working IN your organization, and what percentage of your time are you working ON it?"   – Bobby Albert

41 INFORMAL RESEARCH
You can learn 80% (approximately) of what you need to know about a subject by asking the right ten people the right ten questions in less than ten minutes each. The other 20% of what you need to know takes $100,000+ for formal research.

42 LEADERSHIP—ENEMIES
The three enemies of great leadership are:
1. Fog... Because even a brand new Ferrari can only go about two miles an hour safely in a dense fog.
2. Fatigue... According to the late great Green Bay Packers coach Vince Lombardi, "Fatigue... makes cowards of us all." It also turns us introspective/negative.
3. Flirtations... When you are in a "fog"... become fatigued... you are tempted to flirt with a wide variety of ideas with which you should not be flirting.

43 LEADERSHIP IS
Knowing WHAT to do next...
Knowing WHY that is important... and,
Knowing HOW to bring the appropriate resources to bear on the need at hand.

44 LEADERSHIP—KEY ELEMENTS
85% (approximately) of leadership (from a human perspective) is:
    1. Clear direction
    2. The right team
    3. Enough money
The book Masterplanning calls these three Direction, Organization, and Cash.

45 LEADERSHIP STAR
The five points of the Leadership Star are CARE, HONEST, FAIR, STRENGTHS, and STRESS.

46 LIFE MESSAGE
If you could stand on a platform for fifteen minutes talking to every person alive, what would you tell them?

47 LIFEWORK
Your "LifeWork" is the activity that is worthy of the time, energy, and money you have left in life.

48 MASTERPLAN
A masterplan is a written statement of a group's assumptions about its direction, its organization, and its cash.

49 MEMORY GRID
Anything you have read 100 times you have memorized whether you planned to or not.

50 MENTORING
Ideally, mentoring is a lifelong relationship in which the mentor helps the protégé realize his/her God given potential.

51 MOMENTUM
"CONSIDER that you are in a war to 'CREATE EVIDENCE'—evidence that you are winning, that the strategy is succeeding, that you are building momentum. Fighting against you in this war will be fault-finders who are recording every misfire and telling everyone who will listen. You need evidence to help you gain the genuine support of your colleagues." – Christopher Zikakis

52 MONEY
When you can't figure out exactly what's going on in an organization, watch where the money goes, how it flows . . . from the time it comes in until it goes out.

53 NATURAL EXCITEMENT
What are you really, really, really (yes, you need to repeat really three times) excited about today? This is a non-threatening but very profound question to ask a person. It is also a great question to ask each team member over lunch, dinner, or as a team discussion.

54 NEEDS
There are eight reasons why people do what they do. These are insatiable needs. They are the needs to be:
- ❏ Loved
- ❏ Significant
- ❏ Admired
- ❏ Recognized
- ❏ Appreciated
- ❏ Secure
- ❏ Respected
- ❏ Accepted

We all need all of these. But, different individuals rate them very differently on a 1-10 scale.

55 NEGOTIATION
Negotiating typically implies "more for me . . . less for you!" Never negotiate. Work toward a "triple win" where all three parties involved come away "winning."

56 NEW NORMAL
When major change comes to most people, they keep waiting for things to "get back to normal." When this "I just want it the way it used to be" feeling hits you, or someone you love, remember the phrase a "New Normal."

57 NEW POSITION
What do you really want to preserve, avoid, and achieve?

58 NOTHING
Nothing energizes like a dream
Nothing clarifies like measurability
Nothing intensifies like reducing the time to the target Nothing motivates like results!

59 OPPORTUNITY
"Last year's unexpected success is next year's opportunity." – Dr. Peter F. Drucker

60 ORGANIZATION
Is having a place for everything—and everything in its place.

61 ORGANIZATION—PERSONAL
There are four tools you need to feel personally organized.
1. A "To Do" List
2. A Calendar
3. An Address Book
4. A File System

These can be on a computer or the back of a 3 x 5 card . . . but, you need these four tools.

62 PASSION
"What is your natural passion?" – Chuck Swindoll

63 PEAKING
Plan to "peak" ten years from today. And, each year on your birthday move it out a year.

64 PERSPECTIVE—INTELLIGENCE
Perspective is worth fifty IQ points.

65 PERSPECTIVE—LIFE
You are God's student, not life's victim!

66 PERSPECTIVE—ORGANIZATION
"Where have we been? Where are we now? Where are we going?" – Dr. Ted W. Engstrom

67 PERSPECTIVE—SUBJECTIVITY
To a hammer everything looks like a nail.

68 PLANNING—APPROACHES
There are three approaches to planning:
1. Goal setters' approach
2. Problem solvers' approach
3. Opportunity oriented approach

69 POLICY
Policy is what we always do or, what we never do.

70 PREPARATION
"If you knew, by divine revelation, that you were going to be president of your organization in five years, what would you have to know/do, or become to feel/be ready?" – Mary Graham

71 PRIORITIES
"If you are Noah and the ark is sinking . . . look for the elephants first!" – Preto

72 PROBLEMS—HUGE
What huge problem are you dealing with that you would happily pay 10% of your annual salary to have solved for you?

73 PROBLEMS—SOLUTIONS
"Bring me options/solutions not problems." – Paul Weaver

74 QUESTIONS
If you ask profound questions you get profound answers! If you ask shallow questions you get shallow answers! If you ask no questions you get no answers at all!

75 RAW REALITY
If we just look at "raw reality" where are we?

76 REPORTING QUESTIONS
Once your priorities (measurable goals, problems, opportunities, etc.) are clear, these reporting questions will keep you and your team focused on the boulders:
1. What DECISIONS do you need from me?
2. What PROBLEMS are keeping you from your priorities?
3. What PLANS are you making (which haven't been discussed)?
4. What PROGRESS have you made?
5. On a scale of 1-100, how are you PERSONALLY? Why? (Optional)
6. How can I PRAY for you?

77 ROCKET
What is our "ROCKET"? What is the one project/program/tool/service that everyone likes?

78 ROOT CAUSE
Focus on cause elimination not symptom reduction.

79 SINGLE GREATEST STRENGTH
What is your "SINGLE GREATEST STRENGTH"? What do you DO the very BEST?

80 SINGLE-WORD-FOCUS
What single word captures the essence of your life's direction, organization's focus, next year's focus, sermon, speech, chapter, or presentation?

81 SOMEDAY
"Someday _____ (person/organization) will be a world class _____!"

82 STORY
"What is the story that has magic...a magic title/headline needs to come out of the magic story."
– Bill McKendry

83 STRATEGIC DIRECTION
"A business can tolerate a truly enormous number of errors in detail--if the strategic direction is relevant and correct." – Mr. Richard S. Sloma

84 STRENGTH
"The role of an organization is to maximize the strength of the individual and make the individual's weakness irrelevant." – Dr. Peter F. Drucker

85 STRESS
A high percentage of all stress is caused by indecision or lack of control.

86 STYLE
When someone is doing something in a way that displeases you . . . you need to ask yourself if the way they are doing it is ILLEGAL, IMMORAL, UNETHICAL . . . or, just a STYLE difference.

87 SYSTEMS
"Double the strength of the weakest link in a chain and you double the reliability of the entire chain." – Ed Gruman

88 TIME
"Your true adversary is time; not competition, not legislation, not the economy, but time."
– Richard S. Sloma

89 TIMING—GOD'S
God's timing is perfect . . . even when it differs from our plans.

90 TIMING—WHEN
"It's not what you know. It's not who you know. It's when you know it." – Ed Orr

91 TOOLS
"Any tool a man needs in his business he is paying for, whether he has it or not." – John H. Patterson

92 TRANSITIONS
Transition is a phase in which major encouragement needs to be your focus as a leader. In the middle of a transition keep your team focused on their progress.

93 TRENDS
"Don't only watch the trends . . . watch the changes in the trends." – Dr. Peter F. Drucker

94 TURN AROUND
To turn an organization around in thirty days . . . hire one desperately needed person, fire one visible problematic person, stop something that everyone on the team knows should have been stopped long ago.

95 UNIQUENESS
What is our unique market/ministry position?

96 VISION
"My first responsibility as a leader is to see . . . for if I can't see I'm like the blind leading the blind." – John H. Patterson

97 VISUAL PERSPECTIVE
Draw a picture of how you're feeling right now . . . this gives you "visual perspective" and can snap "fog" into focus very quickly!

98 VITAL SIGNS
What are our seven vital signs (leading indicators of the health of our organization)?

99 VISUALS
A picture is worth 1,000 words . . . and to a visionary, a graph or chart is worth 10,000 numbers.

100 WANT
What do you really want from life?
What do you really need to get there?

101 WORK
An activity is work . . . only when you would rather be doing something else.

APPENDIX A

Helping You Win
Proven Tools to Help in Adjusting to New Life Realities

ASKING TO WIN — *25th Printing*
*Helping You Win By Asking Profound Questions
... 24 x 7 x 365 x Life!*

Would you like to be able to ask exactly the "right questions" at the "right time?" This confidence building booklet fits your pocket, purse, or legal pad to go with you anywhere. Contains more than 100 profound questions to help you deal effectively with life 24 hours a day, 7 days a week, for the rest of your life.

Ten questions to ask in each of the following situations:
1. ASKING ... profound personal questions and avoiding "small talk"
2. BRAINSTORMING ... your way out of a mental "rut" and maximizing your finest ideas
3. CAREER-ING ... when you, or a friend, are considering a career change
4. DECIDING ... when a risky, pressurized, costly decision needs to be made
5. INTERVIEWING ... getting behind a person's smile ... and beyond her/his resume
6. FOCUSING ... or re-focusing your life
7. ORGANIZING ... your life to maximize your time
8. PARENTING ... to raise healthy, balanced children

APPENDIX A

9. PLANNING . . . Masterplanning any organization or major project
10. SOLVING . . . any problem faster with a systematic problem-solving process

This booklet can always be with you to help you win . . .
24 x 7 x 365 x Life!

Also available IMMEDIATELY via download to your laptop or PDA
Ask about imprinted editions for your organization

BOARDROOM CONFIDENCE — *8th Printing*
Bobb Biehl and Ted W. Engstrom
Turns Boardroom Anxiety, Confusion, and Frustration Into . . .
BOARDROOM CONFIDENCE!

Have you ever wished you could sit down and chat with a mentor who would help you to become more confident and effective in your position on the board? Bobb Biehl and Dr. Ted Engstom are now available (with combined experience of 80 years and over 100 boards), to help you! This book is extremely helpful if you are trying to choose the right board members, serving on a board, needing to make board presentations, trying to decide to accept a board position, new to the board, or have been a board member a long while but have never had any formal board training.

This book has become a classic used by thousands of boards world wide.

APPENDIX A

BUILDING YOUR FIRST CHURCH BUILDING
Joe Kimbel
Gives You Confidence in the Building Process – Especially the First Time

Joe Kimbel had over 40 years of experience in church design and construction and was involved in building over 1,200 church buildings. He pastored several churches and was a district superintendent. This book takes you through the step-by-step process of building a church building. In the book Joe shares stories, illustrations, rules-of-thumb, warnings, and encouragement that one would expect from a loving father or a caring mentor. Whatever you do, if you are about to build—especially if you are feeling a bit shaky—GET THIS TOOL!

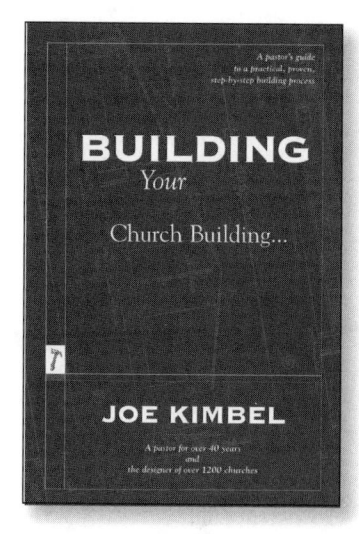

CAREER CHANGE / LIFEWORK
30 Questions to Help You Define Your Next Career Move

Is your current position "just a job," your next "career move," or your "lifework?" This series of 30 questions comes in handy any time you are thinking about the possibility of making a work change. If you are uncertain, these profoundly simple ideas can help. You can also help friends in transition. You hand them these 30 questions, and although they may take hours to answer them all, they will come back with well thought out answers. These questions save hours of time in decision making. Helpful in any

APPENDIX A

career re-evaluating process between the ages of 25-60. A proven resource!

Also available IMMEDIATELY via download to your laptop or PDA

DREAMING BIG!
Bobb Biehl and Dr. Paul Swets
Helps You Define Your Life Dream and Experience an Entirely New Level of Natural Energy.

Do you have the NATURAL ENERGY you would like to have on a day-to-day basis? There are many forms of energy . . . electrical, caloric, caffeine, social, etc. Natural energy for the human being comes from having a clearly defined *life dream*. **DREAMING BIG!** takes you step-by-step through the process of defining / redefining *your life dream*. It is also a great tool to help your entire team tap into its NATURAL ENERGY.

ENCOURAGEMENT Handout
Encourages You, and Your Team, in Life's Predictable Valleys

Every human being "hits a few bumps in the road," has a "blue day" here and there, and occasionally a "bad hair day." In the past 25 years, I have invested approximately 40,000 hours into helping successful executives work their way out of

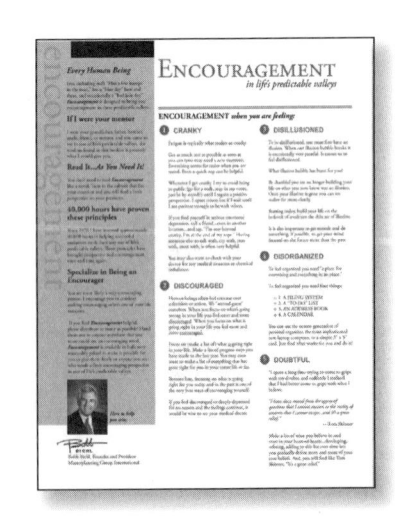

APPENDIX A

life's predictable valleys, and make progress up life's mountains. These principles have brought perspective and encouragement time and time again. If I were your mentor and you came to me in one of life's predictable valleys, the wisdom found on these sheets is precisely what I would give you. These principles can give you encouraging perspective - any time of the day or night whenever or wherever you (or your team) need it - for the rest of your life.

You may want to consider obtaining additional copies to share with family, friends, clients, customers, team members, parishioners, etc.

Also available IMMEDIATELY via download to your laptop or PDA

EVENT PLANNING CHECKLIST — 6th *Printing*
Ed Trenner
Cut Your Event Planning Time in Half

This checklist is designed for those who receive great pleasure from precision and for those who have yet to experience it. The comprehensive 300-point checklist helps you keep from overlooking an obvious question and finding "egg-on-your-face" at the event. Practical, proven, easy-to-use. This checklist gives you a proven step-by-step track for your entire event planning process. Especially helpful if you are new to special events. Ed has conducted several national events over the past 30 years.

Also available IMMEDIATELY via download to your laptop or PDA

107

APPENDIX A

EVERY CHILD IS A WINNER! — *270,000+ IN PRINT!*
Bobb Biehl and Caz McCaslin
Helps You Help Your Child be a Winner!

Healthy children become healthy adults. Caz McCaslin, founder of *Upward Ministry*, is convinced that "Every Child IS a Winner!" *Upward's* ministry had 455,212 children in the FY-2006-2007 year, and the programs included:

- Basketball
- Soccer
- Flag Football/Cheer
- Soccer Camp
- Basketball/Cheer
- Flag Football
- Basketball Camp
- Cheer Camp

This book contains the wisdom and practical "how-to" insights the *Upward* team has learned over the years to help parents know how to develop healthy kids.

FOCUSING BY ASKING —
20th Printing
Pop this CD in on any drive to regain crystal clear perspective on your current situation

Profound questions have helped thousands of people, in all walks of life and at all levels of leadership, focus their lives and teams. This drive time series is set up with 5-minute tracks, covering the following 10 critical elements of leadership:

Personal Focus:
  Keeping FOCUSED
  Keeping CONFIDENT

Team Focus:
  Master ASKING
  Master COMMUNICATING

APPENDIX A

Keeping BALANCED   Master LEADING
Keeping MOTIVATED   Master MOTIVATING
Keeping ORGANIZED   Master PLANNING

Whenever you need to see things in crystal clear focus, remember to pop in this drive time CD on your way to work, your next appointment, or your vacation destination.

FOCUSING YOUR LIFE
A Personal Retreat Guide Based on the Life Blueprint Chart

This is a profoundly simple "big picture" system you learn quickly and can then use to refocus anywhere at any time ... the rest of your life ... in just a few minutes. It works if you have an hour here and there or a long weekend in your very favorite vacation retreat setting. This is a proven "rubber-meets-the-road" book for helping you focus your life. It contains many stimulating, stretching, searching questions / exercises. And every single exercise is designed to help maximize your life FOCUS, core CONFIDENCE, and consistent RESULTS.

APPENDIX A

FOURTH GRADE
The Most Shaping Year of a Human Being's Existence.

This DVD was created for anyone who cares about fourth graders . . . or for anyone with younger children who will soon be in the fourth grade (listed alphabetically):
- Christian education directors
- Elementary school teachers
- Elementary Sunday school teachers
- Grandparents
- Home schoolers
- Little League coaches
- Parents, Psychologists, and other counselors
- Pastors.

On this DVD you will learn why the fourth grade is so extremely shaping, how to take advantage of this very narrow window of opportunity with your fourth grader, and how to avoid serious damage in this highly impressionable period of life. You will understand how at least ten of your leadership "comfort zones" were established in the fourth grade, and how to use this information to help you find a role in life that "fits" you! It is impossible to overstate the importance of this DVD if you deal with fourth graders. It is also an ideal gift for any person you know who does, including any professional from the above list who has a major influence in the shaping of your fourth grader. *DVD*

APPENDIX A

HEAVEN, My Dream of
Jann Bach
A Gift Book Which Will Give Deep Comfort for a Person Grieving the Loss of a Loved One

About 100 years ago Rebecca Ruter Springer had a beautifully vivid dream of what heaven may actually be like. The book has been so helpful that it has been printed many times since then. In this edition, Jann Bach has updated the rather stilted original language to make it easy reading for the person suffering from a devastating loss of a loved one. Reading this book helps the grieving person imagine heaven and their loved one being there at a very real level. It moves the grieving person from, "_____ is GONE!" to "_____ is NOW IN HEAVEN." These few simple words are a major journey in the middle of the grieving process. A major tool for anyone whose responsibility is to help others deal with the grieving process.

LEADERSHIP INSIGHTS
The Best 101 Principles I Know . . . To Strengthen You As a Leader!

You can take advantage of 30+ years in leadership by reading and re-reading these 101 timeless leadership insights. You will find literally hundreds of profoundly simple leadership insights on this one book. Carry it with you and keep reviewing them – soon you will find yourself and your team getting stronger and stronger as you make the insights your own.

Also available IMMEDIATELY via download to your laptop or PDA

APPENDIX A

LEADING WITH CONFIDENCE — *10th Printing*
The Leadership Principles You Need to Lead at Any Level

A wise, proven investment in your own future, covering 30 essential leadership areas including: HOW TO COPE WITH . . . Change, Depression, Failure, Fatigue, Pressure. HOW TO BECOME MORE . . . Attractive, Balanced, Confident, Creative, Disciplined and Motivated. HOW TO DEVELOP SKILLS IN . . . Asking, Dreaming, Goal Setting, Prioritizing, Risk Taking, Influencing, Money Managing, Personal Organization, Problem Solving, Decision Making, and Communicating. HOW TO BECOME MORE EFFECTIVE IN . . . Delegating, Firing, Reporting, Team Building, People Building, Recruiting, Masterplanning, and Motivating. A wise, proven investment in your own future, this series is a lifelong reference.

Also available IMMEDIATELY via download to your laptop or PDA

APPENDIX A

MASTERPLANNING ARROW — *28th printing*
Helps You and Your Team Quickly See:
THE "BIG PICTURE" . . . When you are drowning in detail
THE "FOREST". . . When you feel lost in the trees
THE "SYMPHONY". . . not just a few notes

The *Masterplanning Arrow* teaches you how to quickly sort out the direction of any organization, division, department, or major project you lead — anywhere, at any time, for the rest of your life. *The Arrow* is now available with easy to follow step-by-step instructions, even if you do not order the *Masterplanning* book.

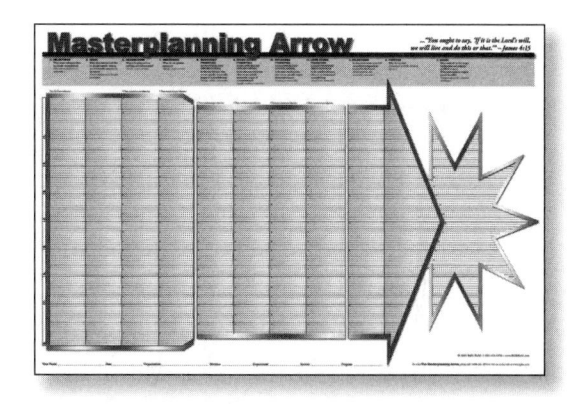

MASTERPLANNING —
4th Printing
Crystalize Your Vision . . . and Get Your Entire Team on the Same Sheet of Music

Masterplanning is an easy to understand step-by-step planning process.
This proven book presents the same process our consulting team has refined in day-to-day consulting practice over the past 30+ years to help clients develop their masterplans.
THE PROCESS HAS BEEN USED SUCCESSFULLY. From "mom & pop" organizations to a staff of thousands. From start-up budgets to hundreds of millions a year. From local churches to

APPENDIX A

international organizations in over 100 countries. From small local churches (under 50) to large area churches (7,000+). From those with no business experience to Harvard MBA's

PREDICTABLE SYMPTOMS WITHOUT A MASTERPLAN. A Masterplan can be likened to a musical score for a symphony orchestra — "Unless everyone's on the same sheet of music, the result will not be pleasant to the ears." Without a Masterplan, expect the following:

- DIRECTIONAL COMMUNICATIONS (internal and external) will be foggy
- FRUSTRATION, TENSION, and PRESSURE will develop because of differing assumptions
- DECISION-MAKING will be POSTPONED because a FRAMEWORK will not be available for clear decisions
- ENERGY and RESOURCES will be wasted because the basic system won't be clearly developed
- FUNDING will be INADEQUATE because of a lack of consistent communication to the organization's constituency
- The ORGANIZATION will suffer because the creative energies will be spent putting out fires

It is helpful to have a clear Masterplan. *Hardcover book – 288 pages*

MASTERPLANNING STRATEGY WORKSHEETS
Double Your Delegating Confidence With One Simple, Proven Handout Sheet

This quick, systematic, step-by-step worksheet helps you think through a solid success strategy for each of your projects. Use these

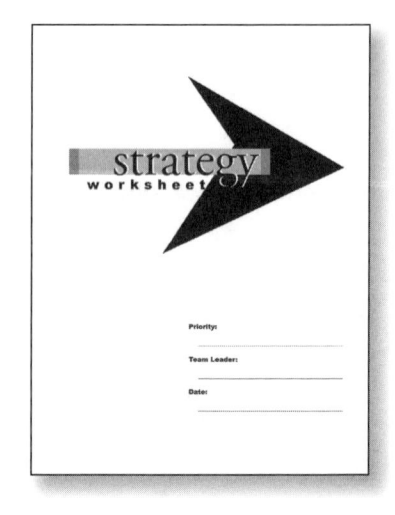

APPENDIX A

sheets to ask each staff member to draft a strategy for turning each major priority into a realistic plan. *Strategy Worksheets* help you spot problems in basic thinking and strategy before those problems become costly realities.   Reviewing staff plans - drastically reduces your risk! *11" x 17" Worksheet*

Also available IMMEDIATELY via download to your laptop or PDA

MEMORIES — *8th Printing*
An Ideal Birthday or Christmas Gift for Your Parents / Grandparents

What makes anything literally priceless? Answer: It cannot be replaced regardless of the price you are willing and eager to pay. Once your favorite people on this earth have gone on to their eternal rewards, whatever memories they have written by hand cannot be replaced, regardless of the amount of money you would be willing to pay. This is one gift absolutely guaranteed to become a priceless family heirloom.

If your parents, grandparents, favorite aunts and uncles, or mentors are still living this is the perfect gift. Written memories become heirlooms for your children's children and are guaranteed to become priceless with the passage of time. *Memories* contains over 500 memory-jogging questions to help your loved one relive and write about her or his life's milestones. It's a beautiful album-type book with padded covers and a binding which opens widely for easy writing. *Memories* is also a "boomerang" gift! You give it to your loved one this year, he or she fills it with memories over the next 1-50 years, then it returns to you as an heirloom for your children's children.

115

APPENDIX A

MENTORING – Book — 5th *Printing*
FEATURED ON FOCUS ON THE FAMILY
Shows You Step-by-Step How to Become a Mentor or Find One

A mentoring relationship can easily add a feeling of 30-50% extra LIFE-LEADERSHIP HORSEPOWER to any person. Without a mentor, a person often feels underpowered, as if not living up to her or his true potential. Ideally . . . mentoring is a lifelong relationship in which the mentor helps the protégé realize her/his God-given potential. This proven book explains clearly what mentors do and don't do, the nature of the mentor/protégé relationship, the most common roadblocks to effective mentoring, and much more. Mentoring is something any one can do . . . but not everyone should do. A successful mentor doesn't require perfection, and finding a mentor is probably much easier than you think. If you have been praying about a way to have your life make a very, very significant difference . . . mentoring may be your life ministry! Hardback, 215 pages

MENTORING – Booklets
An Ideal Handout When Your Group Is Discussing the Topic of Mentoring

This proven booklet gives you many useful how-to steps for forming a mentoring relationship and answers practical mentoring questions with life-proven answers.

Also available IMMEDIATELY via download to your laptop or PDA

MIDLIFE STORM

If You or Someone You Know Feels Lost in the "Midlife Fog," This is a "Fog Cutter"

This hope-filled book contains a crystal clear "Midlife Map" which helps successfully guide you, or a friend, through the very dangerous midlife years. Just because you or your mate is beginning to ask a few midlife questions, does not automatically mean you are experiencing the dreaded "Midlife Crisis." There are three distinctly different midlife phases:
* Midlife Re-evaluation
* Midlife Crisis
* Midlife Drop Out

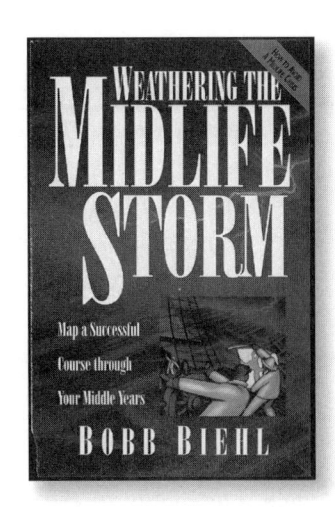

This book addresses each of the three phases with specific step-by-step instructions on how to avoid the pain and confusion of a midlife crisis . . . or if you are already there, how to get out and get on with the rest of your life.

Also available IMMEDIATELY via download to your laptop or PDA

APPENDIX A

ON MY OWN — *7th Printing*
FEATURED ON FOCUS ON THE FAMILY
An Ideal Graduation Gift!

Many adults have said that they wish their parents had taught them these principles before they started off "on their own." Parents, as well as students, benefit from these extremely fundamental leadership principles. If you have been increasingly concerned about your high school or college student's readiness to face the "real world," this book has been written for your son or daughter. These principles will stay with your son or daughter for a lifetime, and they can pass them on to their children's children. *Hardback 338 pages*

PRE-MARRIAGE:
GETTING TO "REALLY KNOW" YOUR LIFE-MATE-TO-BE
Helps You Spot Problem Areas in Your Relationship Before You Say "I Do"

These are the heart-to-heart questions you ask <u>before</u> you say "I Do" to make sure this is the right person for you. This book is a perfect counseling supplement! Assign any couple this pre-marriage book and have them spend several hours discussing the questions. There is a place in each book to mark the questions which are "major sticking points." The couple then comes to you with a handful of clearly defined differences. This book can literally save you hundreds of hours per year of premarital counseling time.

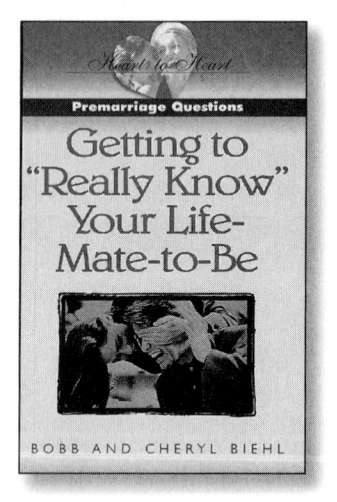

If you have any doubts at all about your upcoming marriage . . . and just want to make sure this is the life mate for you . . . this book

APPENDIX A

can help! This book contains approximately 250 fun questions that will stimulate many heart-to-heart conversations in each of the seven basic areas of life. The book also has steps for resolving disagreements. A very appropriate pre-marriage gift for any friend.

Also available IMMEDIATELY via download to your laptop or PDA

PRESIDENTIAL PROFILE
This Tool Helps Identify and Evaluate Strength and Growth Areas

How would you rate your current president . . . on the 30 dimensions required to be a world-class president? Which of the candidates you are interviewing to be your next president gets the highest rating on the 30-point presidential profile? Are you equipped to be a president? Should you let your name stand? How would you rate yourself as a president on these 30 leadership dimensions? Where do you need to grow to be ready to be president . . . someday? If you have been asking yourself any of the above presidential questions, this easy-to-understand (1-10 scale) profile can be a proven guide for your reflections and your team's discussions and evaluations.

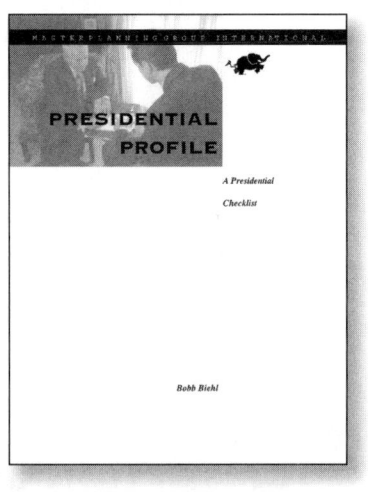

Also available IMMEDIATELY via download to your laptop or PDA

APPENDIX A

STAFF EVALUATION—135
This Is a Strong Track for Your Annual Career Path Discussion with Your Key Staff Members

Have you ever wanted a comprehensive checklist for telling a staff member (in a kind and constructive way) exactly how he or she is doing, on a 1-10 scale, in everything from bad breath to decision making? This is an ideal tool for you to use with those close to you, focusing on 135 dimensions in all. This list helps maximize your staff while concentrating on the positive.

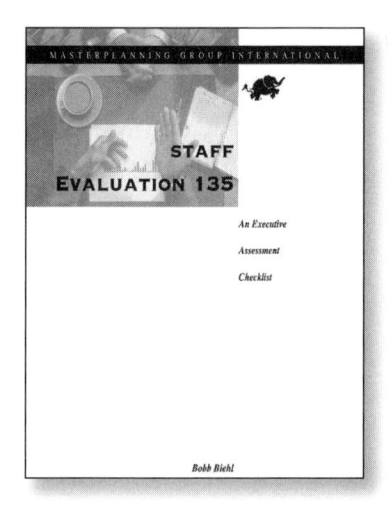

Also available IMMEDIATELY via download to your laptop or PDA

STOP SETTING GOALS
If You, "Hate Setting Goals"... or Know Someone Who Does – This Book Is for You!

"I no longer feel like a second-class citizen!" is the most common reader reaction after reading *Stop Setting Goals*. This book has already freed thousands of readers for life! As a team leader you can reduce team tensions, and, at the same time, significantly increase team spirit by introducing this simple idea at your next staff meeting. Every ten years or so, a simple idea comes along that is so powerful it changes business attitudes forever. This is one of those ideas.

Any leader who understands and implements this idea will make her/his team leader, board and stockholders very happy.

APPENDIX A

TEAM PROFILE — *25th Printing* (Formerly Role Preference Inventory)
This Tool Will Help You, and Your Team, Get "Round Pegs in Round Holes"

The *Team Profile* is a proven way of understanding yourself better. In simple language it lets you tell your spouse, your friends, or your colleagues: **What makes you tick! What turns you on! What burns you out!** The *Team Profile* clarifies what you really want to do, **not** what you have to do, have done the most, or think others expect of you. It is the key to understanding personal fulfillment and is an affordable way of building strong team unity by predicting team chemistry. This profoundly simple, self-scoring, self-interpreting inventory is the key to selecting the right person for the right position, thus helping avoid costly hiring mistakes.

Also available IMMEDIATELY via download to your laptop or PDA

APPENDIX A

WHY YOU DO WHAT YOU DO — 4th *Printing*
Understand Why the People in Your Life Do What They Do

This book is a result of more than 40,000 hours of behind-the-defenses experiences with some of the finest, emotionally healthy leaders of our generation. **This model was developed to maximize "healthy" people with a few emotional "mysteries" still unanswered.**

- Why do I have a phobic fear of failure, rejection, or insignificance?
- Why am I so "driven" to be admired, recognized, appreciated, secure, respected, or accepted?
- Why am I an enabler, leader, promoter, rescuer, controller, or people pleaser?
- Why am I a perfectionist, or workaholic?
- Why are pastors vulnerable to affairs?
- Where am I the most vulnerable to temptation?
- How do I guard against temptation?
- Why do I have such a hard time relating to my parents when I love them so much?
- Why do they sometimes seem like such children?

These and other "emotional mysteries" can be understood and resolved in the silence of your own heart without years of therapy.

APPENDIX A

WIDOW'S WORKBOOK
Dixie Johnston Fraley Keller
If you are a widow or know someone who is, this is the gift that can help.

The Widow's Workbook, A Widow's Bible Study, written by Dixie Johnston Fraley Keller who was widowed publicly while people watched on television a "Lear jet that was out of control." Metaphorically, as her life with her husband was soaring, it all came crashing down. As she picked up the pieces she invites you to join her widow's walk down this winding road.

Learn to live again:
- Loving & Losing
- Grieving
- Giving
- Coping
- Appreciating
- Living on

WRITING YOUR FIRST BOOK
Bobb Biehl and Mary Beshear, Ph.D.
This Simple Tool Can Save You Days in Writing Your First Book

If you have been wanting to write a book for years but still haven't actually started a manuscript, let *Writing Your First Book* be your starting point! Together these two authors have published over 20 books. This is a skeleton outline—no complicated, sophisticated theory or double talk. It is just a bare bones, easy-to-follow, step-by-step checklist to help you become a royalty-receiving author. A wise investment in your own future.

Also available IMMEDIATELY via download to your laptop or PDA

APPENDIX B

Consulting Institute
Your Ability + Our Experience = Your Success

    The Consulting Institute is a one week in depth consultant training experience. It is a place where we make a trade . . . you trade the trial and error phase of your consulting practice for my 30+ years of consulting track record. The Institute is fundamentally a professional accelerator for you as you get started in the consulting profession. You now have over 30 years of experience . . . experience with over 400 clients 40,000 hours of consulting . . . available to help you get a head start in the consulting business. I will be teaching you my very best. The Consulting Institute is what I would teach my own children about consulting. With over 30 years experience, as a personal and organizational development consultant, the principles I teach are those I have proven day after day in my personal consulting practice.

    If you are interested in becoming
- A professional consultant
- A regional manager with a consulting style of leadership
- A trusted / respected advisor to groups

    I'd like to invite you to explore the possibility of attending the Consulting Institute.

www.ConsultingInstitute.com

APPENDIX B

Leadership Academy

*Helping You Get Ready Today —
For What God has for You Tomorrow*

The Leadership Academy is a one week extensive immersion in the leadership tools, processes, and principles that every leader needs at all levels of leadership. These tools apply to the smallest group and to the president of any country. This is the essence of what I have learned about leading from my consulting experience with some of the finest leaders of our generation. This material comes out of 30+ years and thousands of hours of consulting with over 400 organizations. The Academy is a systematic step-by-step understanding of leadership . . . not just a book here and a tape there.

The leadership framework is composed of a teaching notebook and 25 sections including a DVD, a worksheet, and other supplemental handouts for most sections. These 25 tools can be learned in any order. Start where your need is the greatest, and sooner or later you will have completed the entire Academy. The Leadership Academy teaches you 25 tools you can draw on 1000 napkins in informal situations over the next 50 years as others look to you for leadership.

Or, you can teach these tools to your older children, protegés, students, or staff in a more formal setting. The Leadership Academy model is also a life long organizing framework for all of the other information you will learn for the rest of your life . . . in the areas of Leadership, Management, or Life in general.

The Leadership Academy is also available with all of the materials which are included in the one week intensive . . .teaching notebook and 25 DVDs, worksheets, handouts, etc., as a distance learning set. **You are invited to participate in the Leadership Academy — in person or via the Leadership Academy DVD set**

www. LeadershipA.com

Masterplanning Group
Consulting Services — Helping Turn Your Dreams Into Reality

STRENGTHENING CHRISTIAN LEADERS WORLD WIDE . . . is the focus of Masterplanning Group. Our thousands of hours of consulting experience is in four main categories:

* Large and fast growing churches
* Non profit organizations
* For profit corporations
* Government agencies

We are Executive Mentors. Our team has a simple three step process:

1. Find someone we truly believe in
2. Understand where they want to go
3. Help them get there!

We stay on your agenda . . . we don't bring our own. We bring years of experience, processes, principles, and questions to strengthen clients as they move strategically into the future. We bring objectivity that keeps a 50,000 foot objective view of your organization. We then try every way we know to strengthen each and every person on your team . . . to move in the direction of your dream.

www.MasterplanningGroup.com

APPENDIX B

QW

QuickWisdom
Quick Access To Timeless Wisdom . . . FREE!

As an executive mentor / consultant, I have the rare privilege of spending days at a time with some of the finest leaders of our generation. I continue to grow personally, learning more in the past year than I've learned in the five years before it.

Mentoring Realities
In my book Mentoring, I define mentoring as follows, "Ideally, mentoring is a lifelong relationship in which the mentor helps the protégé grow into her / his God-given potential." Realistically, because of schedule pressures, my personal mentoring is limited to a very few individuals. At the same time, I truly want to see friends like you grow into your God-given potential over your lifetime.

Solomon advised, "Get Wisdom."
The search of today seems to be focused on becoming a courageous, charming, powerful, successful person. However, Solomon, who was the wisest man that ever lived, gave us this profound and timeless bit of advice in Proverbs 4:5 . . . GET WISDOM! The focus of QuickWisdom is to help you and your friends be WISE!

Quick Access to Timeless Wisdom . . . 24 x 7 x 365 x Life
Today, it seems that every young leader I meet wants wisdom, but needs it fast. We don't have the time with today's pace and pressures to go to a mountaintop and study ancient manuscripts in Sanskrit. Thus "Quick Access to Timeless Wisdom." Each month I send 2—3 emails . . . free of charge . . . with the very best "wisdom nuggets" I come across during my consulting to help strengthen you and your friends. I want to keep in touch with friends like you and help you,

APPENDIX B

your family, and your team win!

QuickWisdom is 100% free to you – and your friends.

Fortunately, the email technology of today is such that you can enroll 10 friends or 100 to receive the QuickWisdom email (Please pass each QuickWisdom to a friend who could benefit from it). It takes me the same exact amount of time to send you an email as it does to send it to all of your protégés / friends. I want to use my unique exposure to great wisdom to strengthen you and your friends for a lifetime. Thank you, my friend, for telling your friends about QuickWisdom!

To receive these FREE QuickWisdom emails simply visit www.QuickWisdom.com and sign up.

Please send me the following (free of charge):
- ❏ A complete catalogue of Bobb Biehl tools / services
- ❏ An invitation to the Consulting Institute
- ❏ An invitation to the Leadership Academy
- ❏ QuickWisdom

Name _____

Title _____

Organization _____

Address _____

City _____ State _____ Zip _____

Daytime telephone (_____) _____

Fax (_____) _____

E-Mail _____

Contact:
    Fax: (352) 385-2827
    Toll free fax: (888) 443-1976
    Ordering: (800) 443-1976
    Web: www.Aylen.com

Thank You My Friend!

Bobb
BIEHL